BEA GREAT
&
MIND YOUR BUSINESS

30 Days of Empowerment for A Thriving Business

BEATRICE MONIQUE

COPYRIGHT
Mind Your Business & Bea Great
Copyright © 2020 Beatrice Monique Rivers

All rights reserved. No portion of this publication may be reproduced, distributed, or transmitted in any form or by any means, including photocopying, recording, or other electronic or mechanical methods, without the prior written permission of the publisher, except in the case of brief quotations embodied in critical reviews and certain other noncommercial uses permitted by copyright law.

For permission, contact the author: Kingdomstreetzconsulting@gmail.com or call (318)-600-5997

ISBN: 9798663198981

Cover Design, Editing & Formatting by C.L. Ware for Azania Creations LLC Publishing Division

DEDICATION

There are so many people that have helped to shape and inspire me in my journey of being an entrepreneur. This road has had some ups and downs, but it has all worked out for my good. I want to thank every person that has prayed for me and sowed into my life. I want you to know I love you from my heart. I dedicate this book to my younger self, the girl that always knew joy would come in the morning. I want to thank her for being strong and being a fighter.

To my grandmother Lovie Taylor, I know you are so proud of me. Your prayers have carried me through some hard times. I love you and miss you. Thank you for giving me a good example of what a hard-working, godly woman is. I am forever grateful for our time together.

THANKS AND ACKNOWLEDGEMENTS

I want to thank God for all His blessings. He keeps on doing great things for me.

To my amazing parents Michael and Terri Hunt. I love you both. Thank you for being such wonderful parents and grandparents.

To my siblings, I love you. I want to thank Lloyd and Melanie Boudloche. They came into my life at the perfect time and have been so amazing to me. To my mentor PM Global, thank you for sowing into my life. To my 3 beautiful children Briana, Destiny, and Jay, you are my world and the reason why I push so hard. I thank God that I am your mother. It has been my greatest joy. Finally, thank you Stefon. You are the man God sent for me at just the right time. Your love and support have pushed me to become a better entrepreneur. I love you always.

CONTENTS

Dedication 4
Thanks, And Acknowledgements 5
Introduction 7
Loyal To Your Calling 12
Where Is Your Vision? 15
Today Not Tomorrow Stop Procrastinating 18
Bye: Stay Away From Negativity 22
Done With It (Forgiveness) 26
My True Authentic Self 30
Divine Connection 35
You Can Begin Again 39
You Have Been Commanded To Bea Great 43
Rejection Is Protection And Redirection 49
Managing What You Have 54
The Balancing Act 59
It Is In My Hands, So Now What? 63
Organization Is Key 68
The Golden Rule 72
Operating In Excellence 75
The Process Is Not Pretty But It's Profitable 80
By This Time Next Year 85
My Faith Lifts Me Higher Than My Fears 89
Something Wonderful Is About To Happen For Me 93
Keeping Your Momentum 96
Start Your Day With A Praise 102
God Gets The Glory 105
Prayer Is Essential 109
Get Your Mouth Right 113
A Kingdom Business 116
Biblical Wealth And Prosperity 121
Submit Your Work Unto The Lord 124
You Have To Sow In Order To Grow 127
You Will Lose Your Oil Around The Foolish 130
Daily Affirmations 135
Biblical Promises 137

"Mediocrity will never do. You are capable of something better." —*Gordon B. Hinckley*

INTRODUCTION

"Bea Great" is more than a brand, it's a lifestyle and a way of thinking, that will cause you to manifest your true purpose. That is why I wrote this book, because I want to encourage entrepreneurs. The hardest thing about being an entrepreneur is believing in yourself. It's easy for doubt to take root in your heart and in your mind, especially when you see so many people giving up on their dreams.

I want to encourage you to push for your dreams and believe in yourself. The bible says that our gifts will make room for us. So, what that tells me is everything that I need to make it in life is already inside of me, but it's up to me to activate my purpose and calling in life. In 2015, I started using simple positive affirmations in my life. Affirmations are nothing but short statements that give you a positive way of thinking. These statements will affect your thoughts in a positive way. By stating affirmations, you are calling those things that are not as though they are. You are calling attention to your thoughts. You have the power to move your thoughts in the direction that you want them to go. I noticed that once I started saying positive things, I started to feel better about the things that were going on in my life.

I remember the days when I would always say, "I'm tired", "I'm sick", "I'm broke", and when I would say those things, I would feel that way. I would be so down on myself and so depressed. But once I started speaking positive affirmations over my life such as, "I feel replenished", my mind is renewed, all things are working together for my good, my life and business began to take a positive turn. Being an entrepreneur is one of the hardest jobs, you'll ever have.

Today I want to encourage you to be great in everything that you do and speak positive affirmations in your life. Let "I am" become your truth and "BEA Great" become your lifestyle.

Lord Jesus, I thank you that the person who is reading this book will begin to walk in the purpose that you have ordained for their life. I pray this book will speak to their heart and their mind, that it will reach them in the place where fear and doubt abide and give them encouragement and boldness. God, you said in your word that we have not because we ask not, so right now, I ask for a renewed mind and renewed spirit for every reader. Thank you, God, that all things are working together for their good and that they will have the right connections to support their vision. I thank you for my brother or my sister who is reading this book. Bless their hands and make them great. In Jesus' name, Amen.

So, what are you waiting for? Get up and Bea Great!

"You must expect great things of yourself before you can do them." —*Michael Jordan*

1
LOYAL TO YOUR CALLING

Being an entrepreneur is a calling. It's not for the weak or the faint at heart. It's up to you if your business will succeed or if it will fail. When I started my first business, I was deathly afraid; I was afraid of failure and rejection. I can openly say now that I should never have been afraid. God calls us to be bold as a lion, and in business, it takes boldness.

Yes, I'm sure there are other entrepreneurs in your area doing the same thing that you may be doing or selling the same products that you sell, but those people don't have your anointing. Those people don't have your calling. If you are called and anointed to be an entrepreneur, then God will make the way for you.

Being an entrepreneur takes bold faith. It takes perseverance and dedication, and you must be loyal to your calling. Nothing should ever separate you from your dream that God has purposed for your life.

Affirmations

- I am loyal to my calling.
- I will not give up even when times get hard.
- I am smart, successful, and savvy in my business.
- I will create opportunities for growth for myself and my business.
- I am driven by passion and purpose.
- I am a natural-born entrepreneur.
- I am a successful business leader.
- My business is growing in just the right places.
- This Is My Season to be blessed and favored by God
- My business adds value to the community and to the kingdom of God.
- I am dedicated to succeeding in business.
- My business plan is perfect, and it will work.
- I always come up with bright and innovative business ideas.
- I am an expert at everything I do.
- I am bound to be successful in business.

God, I thank you on today for all the gifts and talents that you have given me. I will not disappoint you by hiding them. I will not disappoint you by continuing to sit in the back. Because you have called me to be great. You have called me to be successful. You have called me to change my community and to advance the kingdom of God. I thank you on today for all the blessings that you have given me. I thank you for new ideas, new revelation, and new streams of income. I thank you that I will continue to walk in my purpose and my calling. God, I will be loyal to the vision that you have given me. I will work this vision that you have given me. Even when times get hard, I will not give up. In Jesus' name, Amen.

Reflections, Inspirations, & Strategies

_____
_____
_____
_____
_____
_____

2
WHERE IS YOUR VISION?

Proverbs 29:18 says, "Where there is no vision, the people perish." Your vision is the most important thing that you can ever have. It is your blueprint to the place where God is taking you. Your vision will always need to be in the will of God. The perfect will of God is what's best for us. Your vision will provide a focal point of where you are trying to go. It should always embody all your hopes and your dreams and give you a clear picture of what is to come.

Your vision should be positive, specific, and ambitious. You must see yourself as God sees you, as being the head and not the tail, above and not beneath, a lender and not a borrower. Your vision must be clear to get to the place that God has for you.

Affirmations

- I am inspired with inner vision.
- I have a clear view of my own blessed purpose.
- My vision is far-reaching.
- I am seeing perfectly now with increasing clarity and precision.
- I can see myself as a successful entrepreneur.
- I see clearly through everything that is around me.
- I can see myself manifesting my purpose.
- This is a new day with endless possibilities.
- I can see myself living the life I have always wanted.
- I can see myself healthy, whole, and healed.

Lord, I thank you for a clear vision. I thank you that the scales have fallen off my eyes and that I can see the life that you have ordained and created for me to live. Jeremiah 29:11 says for I know the plans that I have for your life plans for a good future and an expected end. I thank you that my expected

end is greatness and an overflow of blessings. My path is clearing as I walk in my divine purpose, and where you lead me, I will follow. No trap or snare from the enemy will derail me off this path you have set before me. Amen.

Reflections, Inspirations, & Strategies

_____
_____
_____
_____
_____
_____
_____
_____
_____
_____
_____
_____
_____
_____
_____
_____
_____

3
TODAY, NOT TOMORROW. STOP PROCRASTINATING

Have you ever heard the saying, "Do not put off what you can do today"? That is exactly what comes to mind when I think about procrastination. Procrastination is nothing but putting off a task that you can handle and take care of today. A lot of entrepreneurs have this issue. They procrastinate constantly and do not realize that procrastination is the number one dream killer. It will literally suffocate your dream.

A lot of people procrastinate for different reasons. It can simply be because of fear or it can just be out of habit. Sometimes we can start things and then do not push ourselves to finish them. Being an entrepreneur, you must have a strong spirit of running toward the finish line. Getting up every morning knowing that you will press toward the mark of the high calling and finish each day strong. Here are some things that you should do that will help you to stop procrastinating:

1. Set a schedule every day and follow through with it. No matter what happens, keep your schedule being an entrepreneur. You must be intentional about keeping your word. If you tell a customer that you will call them back at 9 a.m., make it your business to keep your word and call the customer back at 9 a.m.

2. Stay organized. Organization is key to keeping up with important dates and appointments. Get a monthly planner. Keep notes in your phone, but whatever you do, stay organized.

3. Get an assistant. You are not Superman. You are not Superwoman. You cannot run a one-person empire. It takes help to BEA Great!

4. Don't overcrowd your schedule. Only take on as much as you know that you can complete in a normal

workday. Having customers wait is bad business. You always want to be timely with all your obligations.

Affirmations

- My time is valuable to me.
- Today, I will take a big step toward reaching my goals.
- My future depends on my today.
- I love taking action.
- I am focused on my goals and I will reach them today.
- I strive for positive change. I know where I am going, and I am capable of getting there.
- I free myself from all negativity that will hinder me from reaching my goals.

God help me to become the person that you have called me to be, a person that is effective in the 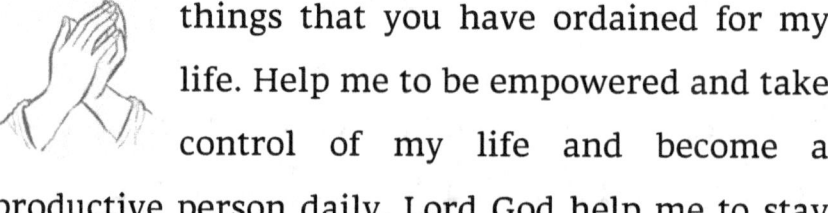 things that you have ordained for my life. Help me to be empowered and take control of my life and become a productive person daily. Lord God help me to stay organized so that I can accomplish the things that you have set before me. I want to make you proud of me and I do not want to waste any time that you have given me because I know that my time is precious. I know that the thing that you have called me to do is just for me to accomplish. So, Lord, please help me to be a better person. Amen.

Reflections, Inspirations, & Strategies

_____
_____
_____
_____
_____
_____
_____
_____
_____
_____
_____
_____
_____
_____

4
BYE: STAY AWAY FROM NEGATIVITY!

Let's just face it, negative people love bringing others down. They are always critical, and they always want to downplay your dream and your vision. Sometimes it can almost seem like that is the only thing they enjoy doing. Negativity is a lethal poison that will sift your dream and kill your business. It is so important that you surround yourself with people that are positive.

Have you ever woken up in the morning and you were having such an excellent morning? Everything was exactly right. The coffee was right. You had a great breakfast that morning. You were full of energy and suddenly, a negative person comes into the room. I like to call them the energy suckers because they literally suck the life right out of the room. These are the types of people in business that you need to run away from.

Not only do they sabotage their own life, but they will sabotage yours as well. Proverbs 13:20 (KJV), says whoever walks with the wise becomes wise, but the company of fools will suffer harm. Negative people will harm you. They will harm your thought process. They will even harm your divine connection.

So today, I want you to look in the circle of people that are around you and start to distance yourself from the negativity. You only want positive people around you in your season of building as an entrepreneur. You want to be encouraged. You want to have people around you who can help you develop into the person that God has called you to be.

Say, "Girl, BYE!" to the energy suckers.

Affirmations

- Other people do not control my emotions, I do.
- I will welcome positivity into my life.
- I am at peace with what is happening in my life and my business.
- I cannot be both awesome and negative. So, I choose to be awesome.
- Obstacles are now falling away.
- My business will run smoothly today.

- I abandoned old habits and all negativity. I choose positive habits.
- I release people and things that no longer serve me and that are negative.
- I choose the content in my life and I choose positivity.
- Do not come over here with ANY negativity. Only positive vibes this way.

God, I thank you for a renewed mind, a renewed way of thinking, and a renewed way of feeling I thank you that today is going to be a great day and every day after today will be even greater. I thank you that all the heaviness that I felt in the past is now gone I feel complete and renewed on today. I will walk in the fullness that you have created for me. Lord, help me to discern the relationships that are in my life. If I am connected to anyone that is bringing negativity to my life, release me from them in the name of Jesus. Lord, help me to keep my energy and my ways in check so that as I do business, I can be a light in the community and in the kingdom of God. Thank you for a new and positive outlook on my life and my business. In Jesus' name. Amen.

Reflections, Inspirations, & Strategies

5

DONE WITH IT
(Forgiveness)

You might be thinking why there is a chapter in this book about forgiveness. I am so glad you asked. You cannot go any further and receive what God has for you until you truly forgive those who hurt you. How many times have I been forgiven? I am sure too many times to count for me. I have never been too proud to say I am sorry, but that has always been easy for me. In my life, I have experienced some real hard offenses, some from people I didn't know very well, and some from people that I knew and loved. The offenses that I experienced from those I didn't know, I can shake them off, and keep going, but the offenses I experienced from the people I loved really hurt me. I would hold on to them. I found myself becoming a bag lady. I could not receive anything great that God had for me because I was dragging all my bags. God took me through a process to cause me to learn to forgive. He allowed me to go through a season of loss and offenses. I had so much hardness and unforgiveness beginning to take root of my heart, I wanted to be free. I had to find my peace without their apology. I had to realize that forgiveness is not condoning the wrong act as if it never happened, but it is simply letting go so you can go on with what God has for you. The word of God says to be kind and compassionate to one another, forgiving each other. Just as Christ has forgiven you. Ephesians 4:32 is the scripture I like to call my freedom scripture because I would say this daily during my season of loss. I want to encourage you to forgive. Let it go so that you can be blessed.

Affirmations

- I release the past so I can step into the future with pure intentions.
- I can move beyond my mistake.
- I can heal from hurt and pain.
- I am worthy of all compassion and kindness life offers me.

- I trade my anger and rage for understanding and compassion.
- I have the courage to heal and become whole again.
- I will treat myself with respect and kindness from today on.
- I lay down the heavyweight of doubt, shame, guilt, and embarrassment.
- I am capable of loving who and what I am.
- I forgive myself so that I can have inner peace again.
- I forgive those who have hurt me, and I let it go in Jesus' name. Amen.

God I thank you that on today my heart will no longer harbor unforgiveness. I am letting go of all hurt and bitterness I ask that you heal my brokenness and fill my empty places. I am letting go of the past so that I can embrace my future. I will no longer look back on the past hurts I will no longer allow the enemy to play tricks with my emotions. I freely allow the holy spirit to take charge of my thoughts and renew my mind in the name of Jesus.

Lord I give you praise for peace and newness in Jesus name Amen.

Reflections, Inspirations, & Strategies

6
MY TRUE AUTHENTIC SELF

What type of entrepreneur am I? Are you a full-time entrepreneur or part-time entrepreneur? Whichever you are? I am sure this has been a long and hard journey for you. Let me be the first to tell you. That you are just beginning. When you are an entrepreneur, you never stop learning. You must constantly fine-tune your craft in your business and stay up to date on all the newest trends.

This is where a lot of businesses seem to fail because they do not stay up to date on what is going on. There is a huge difference between a full-time entrepreneur and a part-time entrepreneur. A full-time entrepreneur is a person that totally depends on his or her revenue from their business. This entrepreneur generally works hard and generally has a high level of stress. A part-time entrepreneur is a person that generally has a normal 9 to 5 job and they run their business on the side on a part-time level. Whichever entrepreneur you are, I want to tell you that it does not matter. You still need a lot of help and a lot of encouragement. If you are a part-time entrepreneur and you are thinking about going full time, there are several things that you must consider.

Will your income be enough to sustain you for at least one year? Is a spouse or significant other supportive of you being a full-time entrepreneur? Is your business valuable and will it bring in the revenue for you and your family? Are you devoted to making sacrifices for your business to work? These are all questions that you must ask yourself before going into full-time entrepreneurship. If you are a full-time entrepreneur, you should always love what you are doing. You must be committed to your business during the ups and the downs.

Whatever you decide, being an entrepreneur can be extremely rewarding and beneficial for your family and for yourself. I am a true believer that following your dreams overcomes everything, it overshadows everything, and it is the ultimate satisfaction when you see something that you can see in your mind manifest right before your eyes. I want to encourage you to keep pushing toward your entrepreneurial dreams. Whether it is full time or part-time, press toward the mark. It is worth it.

Affirmations

- Entrepreneurship is the safest bet to security and wealth. I treasure the freedom my business affords me.
- I appreciate all the lessons that owning my business has taught me. I take entrepreneurship seriously.
- I have the potential and capabilities to run my own business. I can accomplish anything I set my mind on. I am an entrepreneur.

Help me to take my responsibilities of being an entrepreneur seriously. I thank you for every opportunity and every open door that you have given me, and I do not take the blessings that you have given me lightly. I think you, Lord God, that if I am part-time and desire to become full-time, I believe that door will open in your timing and your perfect plan. I will continue to stay focused and fine-tune my business and walk by faith and not by sight. I will not despise small beginnings, but I will rejoice in every moment, every lesson, and every blessing that you continue to give me and my family. I thank you for new ideas and new ways to generate income. I will continue to be ambitious and bold as a lion. I will seek your face daily for divine direction for my business. I cast out all discouragement and negativity and I fill those places with encouragement, zeal, and power in Jesus' name. Amen.

Reflections, Inspirations, & Strategies

_____

_____

_____

_____

_____

Bea Great!

7

DIVINE CONNECTIONS

I must admit that there was a time in my life where I was not as welcoming and friendly as I am now. That had a lot to do with my upbringing. I was raised with parents that were private, but friendly, so that caused me to be more of a private person. I did not allow people into my life and I honestly believe that caused me to not have many friends at first. Sometimes we can block God's plan for our life by not connecting to the right source. Divine connection is so important. In entrepreneurship connection, is important because it's like getting connected to the right power source. If you're not connected to the right power source, then you cannot grow in the way that God wants you to. This week, I want you to focus on divine connections. Try meeting ten new people.

Try saying hi to everyone you see or even giving a nice friendly smile or sparking up a casual conversation. Connection is everything.

During my first couple of years being an entrepreneur, I was so lonely. I remember saying to my sister that it seemed like the more money I made, the fewer friends I had. After years of being in business, I have learned a couple of valuable lessons. First, you must surround yourself with like-minded people, and if they are on a higher level than you, then be a student, not a know it all. I am not saying leave behind friends and family you have known and had your whole life, but it is important to be open and meet new people, gain new insight, and form new relationships. This will help you achieve your goals and objectives, and those new friends can also be open doors for you. I want you to always remember the people that say it's lonely at the top are usually cold, closed off, and unconcerned about others. That is why they are lonely.

The word of God says to show thyself friendly and to gain more healthy relationships and kingdom relationships, you must simply show yourself friendly and be more open to what God has for you. Do not be the entrepreneur that cries out to God for help and when help comes, you reject it because you are so closed off. When God sends help, embrace it.

Affirmations

- I attract success by being my authentic self.
- I manifest everything I desire. I am a magnet for positive energy, good people, divine opportunities, and healthy friendships. I can do it. I will do it just watch me.
- I am ready to open my heart to new friendships and meaningful connections. I am surrounded by people that genuinely love me.
- I am grateful when others extend smiles, kindness, and friendship to me.
- I seek out interactions with people who Inspire and empower me.
- I naturally attract positive relationships in my life. I am a good and loyal person. I develop long-lasting relationships with ease.
- I have good friends and I value them.

Lord, open my heart to meeting new people soften my heart from past hurts and pains that friends and loved ones may have afflicted upon me. I release those things and I lay them at your feet, I will not go back and pick them up again. I ask that you begin to open my eyes for divine connection. Allow me to get connected to the right people at the right place at the right time. Once you open those doors, Lord, help me to be able to recognize that it is in your plan. And your perfect will for my life and my business. I believe that all things will continue to work together for my good because I love you Lord and I am called according to your purpose. I stand on promise of Romans 8:28. I know that you are not a man that you shall lie, and your word will never come back void. I thank you for divine connections in my life in Jesus name Amen.

Reflections, Inspirations, & Strategies

_____

_____

_____

_____

_____

8
YOU CAN BEGIN AGAIN

Everyone experiences failure at some point in their life and, if you want to achieve success, you need to expect failure. Often, when many people experience failure, they will not do what is necessary to pick themselves back up and move on. Instead, most people let their failure get the best of them. They stopped moving forward with their goals, and just gave up. They have closed the door to their dreams. If you want to achieve success in life, you need to be able to push through failure. You need to be able to push through disappointments and you must be able to push through and keep going. When you are a true entrepreneur, giving up is not an option.

You must keep going after what you believe is rightfully yours. If God planted the seed of a business in your heart, then it is up to you to push to make that business manifest. Failure is not an option. The only option is success. Say this with me: I will relentlessly chase after my dream. I will never give up. I will never give in. Failure is not an option. As a matter of fact, it is not even in my vocabulary. I will push through for success. I will push through for the life that I want to live. I will achieve everything I want because I will BEA Great.

Affirmations

- I can push through failure because I am successful. I am persistent and I will never give up.
- I can learn from my mistakes and failures.
- I can keep going no matter what.
- I naturally go after what I want. I am becoming more persistent because I will never quit.
- I will find a way to succeed.
- I will push through failure until I have succeeded.
- I find it easy to overcome setbacks because it is only a setup for a comeback.
- I keep on going because I believe in myself.
- I have an extreme level of persistence.
- I can learn from my mistakes and failures.

God I thank you that I have an extreme level of persistence and I will not give up I will not give in and I will not let go. I will hold onto every gift, every promise, and every dream that you have given me because though I may get weary in well-doing, I will not faint. I trust the vision that you have given me for my life, and I will work hard to see it manifest. I thank you, Lord, that I am turning into the person that you have created me to become. I thank you that I will not give up, I will not give in, and that I am an action taker. I thank you Lord God that I am fearless, and that failure will not overtake me. I thank you for every lesson that I have learned. I will not turn back, and I will not give up. Amen.

Reflections, Inspirations, & Strategies

_____

_____

_____

Bea Great!

9

YOU HAVE BEEN COMMANDED TO BEA GREAT

Jeremiah 29:11 says for I know the plans I have for you because the Lord plans for welfare and not for evil to give you a future and a hope. That is one of my favorite scriptures that has reassured me in times when I felt like I wasn't being great. When I came to realize that God had a plan for my life and that He had a plan for every issue that was going on in my life and my business, for my career and for every choice that I would make it my life, I knew if I simply trusted God, everything would be fine.

I want to tell you today that you have been commanded to be great. Everything that you do, think, and say from this point on should reflect greatness. Being great is more than just a way of thinking. It's a way of doing things, operating in excellence at all times. Being great in business is especially important. It will open doors and you will become a success magnet. Everything that you touch will be blessed.

Being great takes some work and it takes discipline, but anyone can accomplish it. I want to give you a couple of tips that will help you set yourself up for greatness in your business.

1. Set goals to become successful faster. You need a roadmap. You need a concrete way of getting to where you want to go. You need a plan, not just a business plan, but a plan for your business and your life. By setting the bar high, you will always have a source of motivation to work hard and that will only help you to become more successful.

2. You need to establish a routine and stick with it. Most successful people already know this. Now I'm not talking about being repetitious with every little thing that you do every day, but just getting a plan

and sticking to it. If you follow a good routine, it's easier to monitor and keep up with your progress.

3. Having a positive routine in place. You will see quick results and you will be able to see your progress. When you see progress, it only makes you want to work harder.

4. Find a mentor or a business coach. Every business owner and every successful person needs a mentor or a business coach. I even have a business coach. A mentor is someone who is in the same career path as you, but they're further along and they have the proven success record. They can also guide you through things like how to avoid potential pitfalls and how you might approach the next season in your business. Having a mentor can benefit you in many ways and can absolutely help you find success faster than if you had no guidance at all. Don't be the kind of entrepreneur that wants to learn business with trial and error. It will take you ten times longer to get

to the place where you need to be. Don't be cheap. Get a coach, you get a mentor.

5. Streamline your routine. Positive routines can help you advance in your career faster. Let's face it. If you have negative routines and if your life is filled with negativity, you're going to be a slow roll to China. Okay, you need a positive streamline routine. Consider all the things that take up your time that are not helpful to further your career. You know what they are. If you are spending time on social media, cut back that time. It takes discipline to remove distractions, but you'll be able to focus more, which will give you more time.

There are only 24 hours in the day. So, let's make the best of the time that God gives us. Get your routine together. Learn how to say no. This is something I struggle with because I found myself trying to be a people pleaser at times. Saying yes can be gratifying but saying no can be just as gratifying. Sometimes you have to tell people no and that's okay.

That doesn't make you a mean person. That means that you are valuing the time that God has given you. You have other things that you need to do, and you are going to take that time and push for your own purpose, plowing your own vineyard. There is nothing wrong with that. It's okay to say no.

Affirmations

- I live abundantly.
- I am fearless.
- I am a success mad magnet.
- I have a Millionaire Mind.
- I attract success into my life.
- I am a Dream Chaser.
- Everything I touch turns to gold.
- I am reaching my full potential.
- I am focused on success. I am destined for greatness.
- I am blessed and highly favored.
- I am ambitious. Success comes easily to me

I thank you that I am destined for greatness. I thank you Lord that you have put greatness inside of me and that I will continue to birth my purpose. Lord I thank you that I live my life and my business by Jeremiah 29:11. I believe that everything that you have  spoken Over my life will manifest In your time and in your season. I thank you for the success that I will chase after daily. I'm grateful for all the blessings and all the things that you're doing in my life. You continue to do great things for me. All the praise and all the glory and all the honor belong to you. Amen.

Reflections, Inspirations, & Strategies

_____

_____

_____

_____

_____

_____

_____

_____

10

REJECTION IS PROTECTION AND REDIRECTION

I can be honest, one of my biggest fears has often been rejection. I have gone through some hard times of being rejected. One valuable lesson that I have learned in rejection is that most of the time, God was really protecting me from something that I thought I wanted and needed, but it was not in His plan for my life.

Then, there were times when I was rejected, and that rejection catapulted me in a totally different direction for my life. That is why I say rejection is God's protection and redirection. We may not be able to control what happens externally, but we can control our reaction to it. Situations in life and business will come up and you will be rejected, but for every ten no's remember, there's always that golden yes, and all you need is one yes to change the direction of your life.

Nothing ever goes away until it teaches us what we need to know. I remember a season in my life where I had to keep replaying the same thing over and over because I continued to have the same reaction to rejection, and it was rejection on a spiritual level. I was at a place in God and I felt as though it was my time to be elevated. I missed the whole point and the whole purpose of being rejected at that time. I did not understand it. Now, I very well do. It was nothing but God's protection. It was not my time to be elevated. I was not thoroughly cooked yet. It is kind of like if you put a dish in the oven and it does not cook all the way through. Well, once you take it out, it is not going to taste good and it is going to spoil quickly. But if your dish is cooked thoroughly and seasoned right, you can enjoy it and it will last longer. That is how it is in business. You do not want to go out before it's time. You do not want to come out of God's oven before it's time. Stay open to what rejection must teach you. Stay open to those moments when rejection will change the direction of your life. Stay open to the moments in business when you are rejected and turned down. Take those moments and learn from them. Fine-tune the things that you need to do and grow from them.

Every hurdle in business is a lesson.

Do not be the one that has to take the test over and repeatedly until you pass it. There is always something better out there for you. If you are rejected from something, then you are being directed to something else. Stay positive. Keep the faith and keep going. Nothing anyone ever does or says is ever because of you. If you are feeling rejected by a particular person or a business, take comfort in knowing that their actions have nothing to do with you or your self-worth. Rejection is protection. Sometimes we do not know what is in our best interest. I have learned this lesson from business. Trust in God. Trust that God has your back and is guiding you in the right direction. If you are still feeling down about not being accepted by a business partner or by a potential client, remember what God has placed in you is valuable. It is your gift. It will make room for you in God's timing. You must trust that, and you must believe that. You have to know that you are only being redirected to purpose. Purpose far outweighs our own desires.

Affirmations

- I think positively about myself no matter how others may feel.
- I accept rejection with a positive attitude.
- I always take the risk of going after something I want.
- I always say be confident in intimidating situations.
- I am socially confident because God has my back.
- I am free from fear of rejection.
- I am relaxed even though I might be rejected. That is okay rejection is redirection.
- I take risks even when I feel fear.
- I have overcome my fear of rejection.

Lord I thank you for hiding me from the enemy even when at times the enemy was my own wants and selfish ways. I give you praise for the people that walked out of my life and most of all I thank you that even when I was rejected, I kept my faith. When I have been weak your grace has carried me. Amen.

Reflections, Inspirations, & Strategies

_____
_____
_____
_____
_____
_____
_____
_____
_____
_____
_____

11
MANAGING WHAT YOU HAVE

Running a successful business takes more than a good idea as an entrepreneur. You also must have good money management skills. If you want your business to be a true success, you cannot spend every dollar that you make. Having a clear, concise way of how you intend to spend your money will be one of the most critical assets to your business. Look at it in this way: if you cannot manage $300, you will destroy yourself, your business, and your family with $300,000. You must be a good steward over what God gives you.

Being a business owner is a great responsibility, especially if you have employees working for you. These people depend on you and how you manage what God gives you for them to make a living. If you mishandle your finances, it will not only affect you but every one that is connected to you. Before you pay yourself, you should always pay employees. They are the people that take care of you and ensure that your business prospers and thrives. Once you pay your employees, then you pay yourself.

Here are a few principles about growing your business and handling and being a good steward over what God gives you.

1. **Grow Wealth Strategically.**
You must be disciplined in how you handle money. You must be thoughtful and make thoughtful decisions on where your money goes.

2. **Do Not Be Greedy.**
It is imperative that we do not be greedy and miss out on sowing where there are opportunities to sow.

3. Don't Start Your Business Without A Plan.

Your plan is like your roadmap or your GPS. You must have a place of starting and the place of finishing.

4. Be Diligent in Paying Your Employees.

Protect your reputation. A bad reputation is like having a blinking sign over your head. It brings unnecessary attention.

5. Be Honest in All Your Transactions.

This even applies to paying your taxes. You should pay your taxes quarterly. At the end of the year, you will not owe a big sum of money.

6. Be Diligent Over Your Resources.

Remember that Prosperity can be a blessing and it can leave a legacy for your family. It is important to have the mindset that you want to leave generational wealth for your children and your children's children. I often have told my kids that I may not become a millionaire. Of course, I want to and, of course, I affirm myself daily and say it: I will be a millionaire because I want to be great. I always tell them that the blessings on my life will be passed down to them and the next generation and the generation following and on and on. It is important that you always apply Kingdom principles on how to handle your money when it comes to your business.

Affirmations
- I am safeguarding my future.
- I am a successful money saver.
- I know how to spend money wisely.
- I can manage my finances without fear.
- I choose to live a rich life.
- Having money enables me to do good in the world.
- Making money is easy because I choose to live my purpose.
- I am thankful for the abundance in my life.
- I will carefully manage what God blesses me with.

God I thank you that I have an extreme level of persistence and I will not give up, I will not give in, and I will not let go. I will hold onto every gift every promise and every dream that you have given me, because though I may get weary in well-doing. I  will not faint. I trust the vision that you have given me for my life, and I will work hard to see it manifest. I thank you, Lord, that I am turning into the person that you have created me to become. I thank you that I am an action taker. I thank you Lord God, that I am fearless, and that failure will not overtake me. I thank you for every lesson that I have learned. I will not turn back, and I will not give up. Amen.

Reflections, Inspirations, & Strategies

_____
_____
_____
_____
_____
_____
_____

12
THE BALANCING ACT

Trying to balance your family and your business can be quite difficult. Especially when you are a start-up entrepreneur. This is a place where a lot of entrepreneurs struggle. Trying to find a balance with your family and your business can be exceedingly difficult, especially if you are married and you have small children. Now, do not get me wrong. I am not saying to not get married or not have children, but I do believe that you must have a clear, concise balance.

For many entrepreneurs getting started can be intimidating, but it is possible. It is very possible to own a business and a family and have a great balance and a happy life. Balancing a new business and a family can be a huge challenge, especially when they both need your attention. By putting the happiness of your family first, you will surely see that it will make every part of your life and business a lot better.

You must prioritize your health. Too often, new entrepreneurs sacrifice their health while trying to balance their work. You must take care of your body every single day, both mentally and physically. You cannot BEA Great if you are sick and feeling depressed. Take the time that you need rest so you can stay focused and be balanced in your life.

You must work smarter and not harder. Starting a new business requires a lot of time, especially if you are still working your normal 9 to 5 job and trying to have a balance with your family. That can be extremely overwhelming. You must be organized, and you must work smarter. You must manage your time. Do not be afraid to ask for help.

Get the help that you need. Let go of responsibilities that you can turn over to other people; it is okay. If you ask God for help, accept it, and utilize it, period.

Affirmations

- I balance work and family every day.
- I feel balanced and patient.
- I am blessed with a beautiful well-balanced family.
- All my life goals are in perfect balance.
- I always make time just to relax.
- Every day, I achieve greater balance between my thoughts and my actions.
- All aspects of my life are in perfect alignment.
- It feels great to have all aspects of my life under control. I will make time today to honor all areas of my life.
- My vision keeps me focused and balanced.
- My thoughts goals values and emotions are in balance.
- I will make room for myself today in my busy schedule.
- I will remain balanced under extreme stress.

Lord I am so grateful and so thankful for all the many blessings that you have given me. I will not take any of them lightly nor for granted. I ask that you give me wisdom and knowledge on how to keep things in my life in alignment with the word of God.

Proverbs 3:5-7 tells us to, "Trust in the Lord with all your heart and do not lean on your own understanding in all your ways acknowledge Him and He will make straight your paths be not wise in your own eyes fear the Lord and turn away from Evil." So, Lord, I thank you for all the balance in my life. Let me not lean to the left or the right but keep me in alignment in all my ways. Amen.

Reflections, Inspirations, & Strategies

_____
_____
_____
_____
_____
_____
_____
_____
_____

13

IT IS IN MY HANDS, SO NOW WHAT?

You have officially launched your business, but you have no idea what to do to keep your business going, to keep your customers coming, and to keep your revenue growing. So many people have this struggle when they first become an entrepreneur. It is like you've learned how to drive and now you need the directions on the best way to get from point A to point B.

This is where marketing and scalability come into play. Depending on the type of business that you will have, marketing will be a critical component of being great in business. You will soon see that your biggest supporters will be people that you do not even know. Yes, family and friends may support you, but I want you to keep this scripture in mind. Luke

4:24 says, "Truly I tell you no Prophet is accepted in his hometown."

That says it all in the life of every entrepreneur. My biggest supporters have generally been people that I did not even know. Yes. I have had tremendous support from my friends and families, but some of the biggest I have received has at times been from people that I do not even know.

Depending on the size of business you have in the market that you serve, that will determine what type of marketing you will need to do. If you are more in a franchise type of startup, you will need a commercial type of marketing. If you are more into a home-based, small type of business, you will more than likely need to depend on social media type of marketing. A good marketing plan for small businesses will include a website, a blog, and some local mixed type of social media marketing. These marketing tactics tend to give you more bang for your marketing buck.

If you are a home-based type of business, local word-of-mouth can especially be important. Get connected to a few bloggers that have the same type of niche that you do. Remember that divine connection is everything. Get around people that are doing the same thing that you are doing.

Put checks and balances and systems in place that will ensure your success. Get everything automated; that's emails, websites, appointments, and settings. Be sure that all of these things are automated. You want to work smarter, not harder. There's great satisfaction when your business starts generating revenue and it's running smoothly. Don't give up until you get to that place. Will you have some bumps in the road? Yes, but it is possible. Success is extremely near. Keep going. You are doing great.

Affirmations
- I handle success with grace.
- I am always attracting abundance.
- I am grateful for what I already have and for all I will receive.
- I am fully supported making money doing what I love.
- Whatever I put my mind to achieve.
- My faith lifts me higher than my fears.

*L*ord I Thank you for all the amazing and wonderful things that you are doing in my life in the season. I thank you God, for your grace and your love and kindness that you show to me every day of my life. I thank you for being a great God. You continuously look out for me and allow all things to work together for my good. You have blessed me with new ideas and new streams of income with this amazing business. I know that anything that you give me, you will make a way for it. I thank you for placing everything in my hands at the right place and at the right time. Continue to lead and guide me. Give me divine wisdom and knowledge to be the entrepreneur that you would have me to be. In Jesus' name. Amen.

Reflections, Inspirations, & Strategies

_____

_____

_____

14
ORGANIZATION IS KEY

There is nothing worse than trying to find something on your desk with piles and piles of paper. Many entrepreneurs suffer from a lack of organizational skills. Having your business bills and your personal bills mixed can become a complete nightmare. Being organized as an entrepreneur is such a critical part of your success.

It is best to have an "out with the old, in with the new" mentality. Anytime you're finished with a project or paper, it's best to scan it or file it and get it off your desk. Try to keep your workstation clean and organized and purge what you don't need. Only use one calendar. If you are the type of person that still likes to use a paper calendar, that's fine, but only use one. If you are more of a tech-savvy person, it is best to organize your calendar through your email. This will give you updates on the times and places where you need to be. Make a note on your calendar one week ahead of any event about what you need to do for that event. If you need to bring something or if you need to prepare a presentation, it is always best to do it beforehand. A last-minute prep is always the worst. It leaves room for too many errors. You need to be open to change and in touch with your own strengths and blind spots. Adopting better organizational systems will help you greatly.

Take today to make your workspace a positive space, a space where you can think freely and not feel cluttered. When you feel cluttered, your mind cannot operate appropriately. For instance, I am a visual person, so I have to see things. There are times when I may have a lot of paper on my desk, but at the end of the week, I take time to purge everything so I can start fresh the next week. You cannot be great with things all over the place. Get your business organized.

Affirmations

- I am great at managing and organizing projects.
- My mind is sharp and clear, and I find it easy to find everything. I need to complete every test today.
- I am a responsible person who was organized, and I am managing my time well. I love being organized and I find it extremely rewarding.
- I am confident and organized because everything is in its place.

God I am so grateful that you have entrusted me with being a kingdom business owner. Help me to stay organized and operate in excellence at all times. I give you the praise for all the blessings and the doors you continue to open for me in my business and my life. Every door you open for me I will run through it with a renewed mind and my heart and hands ready to receive what you have for me. In Jesus' name Amen.

Bea Great!

Reflections, Inspirations, & Strategies

15

THE GOLDEN RULE

This is a rule that we were taught as young children: Do unto others as you would have them do unto you. I can say that in my years of being in management and an entrepreneur I have always tried to be mindful of how I treated people. I have tried to treat people with dignity and integrity. Now, do not get me wrong. Sometimes, people will push you, but it's always important to understand that everyone is not called to be in leadership or an entrepreneur. Those of us that are called must always follow the Golden Rule: **Make people first.**

Think of others first and just treat people how you want to be treated. When you have customers and employees, they should be the focus. As a business owner, you should always be mindful of how you treat those people. My motto is, "I will not treat an employee nor customer in a way that I would not treat my own family members or want to be treated." Respect goes a long way in business. Remember, people will spend money with you if you have great customer service and always over-deliver and exceed their expectations.

Affirmations

- I will treat people the way that I want to be treated.
- I will treat others with dignity and respect because that is the way I want to be treated.
- I am a beacon of light and I will only give off love and positive energy on today.

Lord Jesus I thank you that, you are such a forgiving and loving God. I thank you for your compassion and your generosity that you continue to show me every day. I ask that you create in me a clean heart and renew a right spirit within me, and that you continue to shine your light upon me. Soften my heart so that I can treat people the way that I want to be treated. Allow me to be compassionate and empathetic to the things that are going on in people's lives. Help me to discern how to operate and pray for the people that you have put me in charge of. I thank you for the opportunity of leadership that you have given me. I will not take that for granted. I want to honor you by valuing the blessings that you have given me and by treating others the way I want to be treated. In Jesus' name. Amen.

Reflections, Inspirations, & Strategies

_____
_____
_____
_____
_____
_____
_____
_____

16
OPERATING IN EXCELLENCE

Having a spirit of excellence in business will open the door for God to get the glory out of everything that you do. Even if you do not yet have everything that you need for your business, live your life with the conviction that your best can always get better because God is in it. That is having a spirit of excellence. Using what you have to the best of your ability and using it fully, is all God really wants from us.

Here are a few things that you will need to operate in excellence:

***Having Good Character**
Character is determined to do what is right no matter what the cause. Your character is more

important than your reputation. Your character is what you really are. Your reputation is only what people think you are. Every day, we are presented with opportunities to sin and to resist temptation. Daniel proved that we can live a clean life even in a corrupt culture. There is always an escape.

* **Conviction**

Conviction often involves doing what is not popular or not doing what is popular. Conviction means you have set boundaries for your life. Conviction is especially important in business. This means that you will not do any and everything to make money, but you will have a standard for your business and for your life.

* **Courage**

Jesus states in the bible to, "Be of good courage for I have overcome the world". If you have courage you can overcome obstacles and opposition in your business. It will take courage to step out on faith and be an entrepreneur, but always remember that God has given you the spirit to overcome anything.

* Consistency

Success usually results from a lifetime of diligence, discipline, and wise decision making. The definition of insanity is doing the same thing and expecting a different result. If you want to be successful in business, you must be diligent and disciplined. You must work when everyone else is sleeping. While everyone else is having fun, you must be working. It takes commitment and discipline to birth the vision that God has given you.

Affirmations

- I am disciplined and diligent in operating in a spirit of excellence daily.
- I will consistently operate in excellence and integrity in my life and my business.
- I have purposed in my heart that everything I do in business, in my family, and with my walk with the Lord, will be with a spirit of excellence.

- My character is impeccable, and my integrity is above reproach because I am walking in the likeness of God.

Jesus, I thank you that I continue to walk in the spirit of excellence Lord. I ask that you continue to be a lamp unto my feet and a light unto my pathway, that I will be a business owner of character and integrity, that I will stand up for what is right in my business in my life, and in my community. I pray that I will continue to be a beacon of light to shine, so that people can see that Christians do operate in integrity in their business. I thank you that the spirit of excellence continues to reign over my life in every area of my life and that you will continue to get the glory from my life in Jesus' name. Amen.

 Reflections, Inspirations, & Strategies

_____
_____
_____

Bea Great!

17

THE PROCESS IS NOT PRETTY BUT IT'S PROFITABLE

The process of starting a business can be very gratifying and stressful all in the same breath. I want to share with you a few steps that can make the road a lot smoother for you transitioning from working a nine-to-five to being an entrepreneur.

Be Inspired.

You should be inspired by the business that you want to start. It should not be anything that is daunting or horrible or makes you feel sick to your stomach. When you think about your business and the thing that you were created, destined, and purposed to do, it should give you butterflies and cause a leap in your spirit. If you have those feelings, then this is what you are destined to do.

Educate Yourself

I am all for college education, but I can say that I have made it through life with the favor of the Lord. Sure, a lot of people go to school to get an education and I encourage that, but an education can never replace God's grace and His favor.

Network.

It is imperative that when you are starting a business that you get around people that have business knowledge and that may even be doing the same thing you are doing. Starting a business with no knowledge of what you are doing is a recipe for disaster. Do not be afraid to ask questions. The only dumb question is the question that was never asked.

Research and Start A Business Plan.

The bible says without a vision the people will perish. You have to have a business plan and research. This is one of the most important elements of business that people tend to skip over. Just because you see one person being successful in the area of business that you want to enter into doesn't mean that area of business is for you. Do your research, have a plan, and be sure that your plan fits with God's plan for your life.

Determine Your Market.

Not everyone will support you. Not everyone will buy your product, but your tribe is out there. Find your market, find your niche, and stay in your lane.

Following these steps can make your journey into becoming an entrepreneur so much smoother. It is a process. There are some steps that you cannot skip. In the end, if you do the work, you stay the course, and you operate your life and your business under kingdom principles, you will win. Yes, the process is hard at times, but the end reward is worth it.

Affirmations

- I am firmly on the path of achievement.
- I plan my work and follow through with my plan.

- I will transform obstacles into opportunities with grace and creativity.
- I visualize the results and benefits of my goals.
- I will prayerfully and powerfully if vision what? I know God has promised me.
- I am destined to achieve because I am a child of purpose.

Lord Jesus I thank you for the process that you are taking me through in my business and my life. I know that all things will continue to work together for my good. I believe that you have called me to the marketplace for such a time as this and that my gifts will continue to make room for me. I believe that I am walking in divine favor, and that you will withhold no good thing from me. So, as I go through this process, I ask that you give me strength to endure, and that I endure this process as a good soldier and that you will continue to get all the glory out of my life as I began this journey as an entrepreneur. In Jesus' name, Amen.

Bea Great!

Reflections, Inspirations, & Strategies

18

BY THIS TIME NEXT YEAR

I am going to share with you something that I often share with most of my clients that I coach. This affirmation is one of the most powerful affirmations that I have ever used.

By this time next year, is an affirmation that I use daily. I have it written on my bathroom mirror. I have a list of things that I am believing God for, to happen by this time next year. I say that list of things every day and I have watched how God has caused my faith to grow daily. I have watched how each one of those things on that list has manifested in my life. I want to encourage you to use this affirmation.

Romans 4:17 talks about calling those things which are not as though they were. That translates into God creates new things out of nothing. So even if you feel like there is nothing there or if something has died, God can make something out of nothing.

By this time next year, I believe that you will be walking in divine destiny, that you will have every promise that the Lord has promised to you, and your business will be flourishing.

Affirmations

- By this time next year, I will be debt-free.
- By this time next year, my business will be doubled in size.
- By this time next year. I will have triple the number of clients and customers that I have now.
- By this time next year, all things that I feel that are a problem in my business will be solved and running smoothly.
- By this time next year money will no longer be a problem for me.

Lord Jesus I thank you, that by this time next year the things that are troubling me or hindering me from moving forward in my purpose and my business will no longer be a problem for me. I believe that you will continue to make all things new and every crooked path straight and every narrow pathway widen in the name of Jesus. I thank you that every area that I felt was dead in my business and in my life, you are now breathing new life into it. I believe that by this time next year, I will be walking in divine favor and my business will be flourishing in Jesus' name. Amen.

Reflections, Inspirations, & Strategies

_____
_____
_____
_____
_____
_____
_____
_____
_____
_____
_____
_____

Bea Great!

19
MY FAITH LIFTS ME HIGHER THAN MY FEARS

Walking by faith and not by sight sometimes can be difficult. It is one of those things that is easier said than done. There have been times in my walk with the Lord and being an entrepreneur that I literally felt like everything was falling apart all around me. I felt like I was holding a handful of wet noodles and no matter how hard I squeezed or held on tightly, something would fall through my fingers. Walking by faith is something that you will hear a lot about in church, but you will not necessarily hear this in business. As an entrepreneur, at some point, you must believe in an idea or concept that had no proof or evidence that was going to work when you decided that you will start your business. It was a 50-50 chance that it would or would not work. That is walking by faith and not by sight.

It is so important as an entrepreneur to not fear failure but to have faith. So many people fear failure that they do not start a business and do not try any new concepts They never get out of their comfort zone. You must walk by faith. Know that God has given you everything that you need. You have gifts and talents locked inside of you that He wants you to utilize. If God did not want you to use them, He would not have given them to you.

Walking by faith means that you will continue to cling to the dream God has planted in your heart, even when you have been discouraged or things may not be working out the way you want them to. Cling to the plan and the dream that God has given you. God is not a man that He shall lie. If He promised you, He will do it!

Affirmations
- ♦ I firmly believe the word of God that I am a person of faith.
- ♦ I am grounded rooted and settled in faith.
- ♦ My faith produces substance and brings to pass with the evidence of what I speak in faith.

- I have mountain-moving faith that will remove all hindrances.
- I affirm there is no lack or deficiency in my life because my faith is in God.
- I gathered myself up daily with the shield of faith.

Lord I just thank you on today and ask that I be strengthened to walk by faith and not by sight. I will please you each day with my obedience as my faith is elevated daily. No matter what the enemy throws my way or how things look, I will stand on the promises that you have given me, and I will continue to walk by faith and not by sight. I will not focus on things that my natural eye sees. These things are just temporary, and they are subject to change according to the word of God that I speak. I will focus my attention on things that are unseen in the spirit realm that shall stand forevermore. I trust you, God. I know that you will cover every trap and every snare that the enemy sends. So, I will continue to walk by faith and not by sight in Jesus' name. Amen.

Bea Great!

Reflections, Inspirations, & Strategies

20

SOMETHING WONDERFUL IS ABOUT TO HAPPEN FOR ME

As a believer and an entrepreneur, you should always walk in the spirit of expectation. Our expectation of God should be a posture of both thankfulness and expectancy.

In Philippians 1:6, God affirms that we should be confident and know that He will complete the work that He has already started in us. He further states that it will be complete until the day of Jesus Christ. This means that we should always be walking in expectation. Being confident in the Lord is what drives our expectations. Having a spirit of expectation in business is so important. Always expecting that great things are going to happen to you in your business and having a positive outlook on how things are going in your business is important.

When you have a spirit of expectancy, that is when you will start to experience a breakthrough. The Bible says that we have not because we ask not. If you are not asking for something, then you are not expecting anything. On today, I want you to have a spirit of expectancy. Expect that something wonderful is about to happen for you in your business.

Affirmations

- I expect lavish miracles and blessings to unfold in my life today and I am grateful.
- I know that on today only good things will come my way.
- I am great yesterday. I am better today. There is nothing that will stand in my way.
- Something awesome is coming my way.
- I am allowing this day to be a date of celebratory blessings.
- I anticipate that today tomorrow and every day will be a great day because I said so.

Lord Jesus I thank you, that on today I walk with a spirit of expectancy and I am only expecting great things. I know that I am your favorite child, and I know that you want more than anything to shower me down with blessings. So, today I empty my hands so that you can fill them up. I expect an overflow, I expect abundance, and I expect to be exceedingly blessed today and every day. I thank you for all of the blessings that you are giving me, and I will utilize every opportunity to give you the praise and the glory in Jesus' name. Amen.

Reflections, Inspirations, & Strategies

_____
_____
_____
_____
_____
_____
_____

21

KEEPING YOUR MOMENTUM

It is always exciting to start a new business, but there will always be some ups and downs in your business. It is important to keep your momentum. You must strike the iron while it is hot. You will hit an unexpected bump or two or sometimes even three. You may even become stagnated and overwhelmed. The next thing you know, you are frustrated and confused, and your momentum comes to a screeching halt. This can be a huge challenge for an entrepreneur. Keeping your momentum will help to sustain your revenue and your brand in front of people's eyes.

Usually, the big questions are how do I keep up the growth and how do I continue to attract new clients? Here are some tips that I want to give you to keep up your momentum.

1. Make helping customers your number one objective. Once you lose sight of the importance of helping customers day after day, you lose sight of your business. If you have a customer-based business, helping customers and customer satisfaction should be number one on your list of priorities.

2. Enhance your online experience for your customers. People buy what they want, but they must know how to find you. Being online and having a mainstream website is crucial to keep up your momentum. You must keep up with the trends and the times. You do not want your customers to always have problems on your website, so be sure to have help in that area. Having an IT person on staff is critical.

3. Keep setting new goals. Setting goals for your business helps everyone to see where the business is going. It helps people have a roadmap to where they are headed. Make collaborative goals and collaborative processes for your employees so that everyone will be able to have a say on any vital issues that may affect the business. Create goals that are in alignment with your core values and your personal vision for success. Do you really need to create a seven-figure business to be successful? No, you do not. But if you do not have goals you cannot even get to two figures.

4. Take double steps. Sometimes you must identify what steps you must take. But once you identify that take that step take double steps. Keep going. But be careful not to bite off more than you can chew do not expect yourself to take Giant Steps the end up causing you to procrastinate instead of moving forward. Take Little Steps but take double steps.

5. Celebrate along the way now this Is something that every entrepreneur must be so careful about it is good to celebrate your victories. But after you celebrate jump on the next project reward yourself for staying on course acknowledge, the small wins along with the way to the bigger goal and do not underestimate the power of Celebration to keep your momentum going. It does not matter if it is a small victory or an exceptionally large one celebrates but once the celebration is over. Move on keep your momentum going.

Appreciate support. There is not a successful entrepreneur out there who is done it all by themselves. We all need support and it is important for us to take care of the people that take care of you. When people feel valued and understood and supported, they tend to work harder for you. Appreciate the people that take care of you.

Affirmations

- ♦ I am so excited about the momentum I am gaining. I am moving forward in my life easily and effortlessly.

- Every day my life gets better and better.
- I have so many new clients. I can barely keep up.
- So many amazing things are outside of my comfort zone.
- Things just keep working out for me.
- I will push myself harder and harder each day because I am great.
- I am gaining speed and gaining more momentum each day.
- With every goal I complete, I am one step closer to gaining more momentum.
- With every goal I complete, I am one step closer to my divine destiny.

God, I thank you for all the blessings that you continue to give me day after day. I thank you for the speed that you have given me to race toward my divine destiny. Lord, I do not want to move too fast, but I also do not want to move too slow. I believe in your word when you said the steps of a good man are ordered by the you. Lord, Jesus order my steps! Take me at the pace that you have for me to go. I trust that you will withhold no good thing from me. As I pray this prayer, I can see my hands filling up with blessing after blessing. Continue to be the light. Continue to be the lamp at my feet and the light of my pathway. I trust you as you lead and guide me in Jesus' name. Amen.

Reflections, Inspirations, & Strategies

22

START YOUR DAY WITH A PRAISE

Starting the day with positive morning affirmations can help you improve any area of your life. Whether you want to make more money, forgive yourself or become successful, they can help. Whether you want to make more money, forgive yourself or become successful, they can help renew your mind daily, and keep your focus on the journey of being an entrepreneur that God has assigned for your life. I am a firm believer that praise gets the attention of God. This is why I start every morning with a praise and a grateful heart. Before you pick up your phone to return calls and emails, before you start the day, get in your quiet place alone with God and give him a few moments of your time. This will renew your mind for the day and enable you to tap into what God has for your life and your business. Be intentional about the time God gives you. Do not make excuses for lost time. Simply be intentional and reclaim your time in the morning and spend it with God.

Affirmations

- I am excited to start the day.
- Today is a beautiful day.
- I am happy and full of joy.
- I attract abundance and wonderful things.
- I am surrounded by beautiful people.
- Nothing will stand in my way of having a great day.
- I am grateful for all of the wonderful things in my life.
- Thank you for blessing me with good health.
- My heart is filled with love and joy.
- I radiate positive energy to all of those around me.

God, I commit my mornings to you, and I give you the praise for another day. This is the day that the Lord has made, and I will always rejoice in it. I thank you for the joy and peace that you give me each day. I am so grateful for your love and how you just keep on looking out for me. I will take advantage of the time and this prosperous day that you have given me. I will use it to honor you and bring souls into the kingdom. You are the potter and I am the clay. Have your way in my life, family, and business. I expect great things on today and every day in Jesus name Amen.

Reflections, Inspirations, & Strategies

_____

_____

_____

_____

_____

_____

_____

_____

_____

23

GOD GETS THE GLORY

Christian entrepreneurs can bring light into an industry that desperately needs it. The marketplace needs more Christian entrepreneurs that are willing and ready to step out on faith. I have come to discover that many believers don't really want to do business because they've seen some questionable business practices, but there are those of us who feel the Lord is tugging and pulling at our hearts to own a business. This call must be answered and never should be ignored.

Honoring your business by doing business God's way is the perfect way that God will get the glory out of your business. Having a successful thriving business where you operate in Integrity will always glorify God your business. It is your instrument to glorify God and it can even be used to bring people into the kingdom of God.

It is important to keep your business covered in prayer. Keep your heart in the right place and have a humbling presence before the Lord. Your business should be a beacon of light that is used to draw people from the world into the kingdom of God. Therefore, you should always operate and love and integrity and all times in your business. This should be toward your employees and your customers. Anyone that God has given you charge over you has influence over and that should never be taken lightly.

In all things that we do in business, we should do it to glorify God. Once you get that mindset then God will open the windows of heaven and pour you out a blessing that you will not have room to receive. It is not about you getting the glory, but God gets the glory.

Affirmations

- God has great things in store for me.
- My mind is renewed. My heart is restored, and I will operate in a manner that God will always get the glory. I can do all things through Christ who gives me strength.
- My life is full of gifts blessings and joy, and I give God all the glory.
- My life and my business bring honor to God.
- I am not a victim. I am an empowered person and I give God all the glory.
- My business and my life are filled with love. Peace joy happiness and prosperity.
- I am proud of everything I have accomplished, and God gets all the glory.

Lord I thank you for the influence and responsibility you have given me with my business. I give you all the glory for the lives that I will touch and the people I will draw by operating in my divine destiny. I ask that you give me wisdom and knowledge to stay focused and stay on the path that

you have for me. Allow me to see and discern the plans and tricks of the enemy before they even happen. I pray that my business and my life bring glory to the kingdom of God in Jesus' name Amen.

Reflections, Inspirations, & Strategies

_____

_____

_____

_____

_____

_____

_____

_____

_____

_____

_____

_____

_____

24
PRAYER IS ESSENTIAL

Being an entrepreneur can be an incredible tool that God can use for his kingdom. Because of that, praying for your business and how you will handle this huge endeavor should be at the top of your to-do list. The Bible says that we should pray without ceasing. This principle should always be applied to your business and how you operate in business.

Having a close relationship with God will strongly affect how you handle the ups and downs in business. For the past several years, I have always started my mornings out with prayer and meditation. I find that if I skip this very critical part of my day, most of the time if a hiccup does happen, I react to it very differently than if I had taken that time with God that morning. So, I want to encourage you to always start your day off with time with God, with prayer, affirmations, and meditation. Prayer is essential in running a successful business. It is just as essential as managing what God gives you as having good credit and paying your bills on time. Prayer should be just as important as the air you breathe. Spending time with God is your lifeline.

Here are a couple of things that you should pray for your business:

• You should ask God to give you a clear and concise understanding of ownership. It is one thing to say that you are a business owner, but it's another thing to understand your divine purpose in owning that business.

• Everything you do should be to glorify and edify the kingdom of God. Your business should do those things. You should pray for new ideas and new streams of income. My goal has always been to make money in my sleep, and that has happened for me by having between seven to nine streams of income. This should be the goal of every believer and every entrepreneur, period. You should pray and ask God to give you creativity and new ways to make money.

• Say yes to the right opportunities and no to the wrong connections. Saying yes to the right opportunities can be as critical as taking your next breath. Some opportunities will only be presented to you once.

• You need the right connections. Having bad connections can make or break your business. Connecting to the wrong person in your season can delay you and sometimes it can destroy you. You should always use discern about placing people in your life, especially in your season of reaping. Always ask God to give you clarity on every decision that you will make in your business. Remember, in all things give thanks and, in all things, give God the glory.

Affirmations

- God is doing immeasurably more in my life than I could ever imagine.
- I live by faith and not by sight.
- God is my refuge and strength always ready to help me in times of trouble.
- The love of God flows through me. I am his and he is mine.
- My business abides in God and I abide in him.
- I am a prayer warrior and God continuously answers my prayers.

Lord may nothing separate me from you today. Teach me how to choose only your way today so each step will lead me closer to you. Help me walk by the Word and not my feelings. Help me to keep my heart pure and undivided. Protect me from my own careless thoughts, words, and actions. And keep me from being distracted by MY wants, MY desires, and MY thoughts on how things should be. Help me to embrace what comes my way as an opportunity rather than a personal inconvenience. In Jesus' name, Amen.

25
GET YOUR MOUTH RIGHT

Speaking positivity into your business can be one of the most vital things that you can do for your business. The Bible says that life and death are in the power of the tongue. I like to say that life and vitality are in your tongue for your business.

It can be difficult to make the most out of your life and out of your business when you are constantly talking yourself out of success. It can already be discouraging when you feel like people are not supporting you. So, there will be times in your business that you will need to be your biggest cheerleader.

I like to reference the story of David in the bible, how he came back from battle and had to encourage himself in the Lord. You will need to apply the same principle to your business daily. You will need to encourage yourself in the Lord.

Having positive self-talk and reprogramming the way you feel about your life and business can set you free from negative thinking. You should start these talks with yourself every morning. The first thing that you should say out of your mouth should be something positive, like Lord I give you all the praise for waking me up this morning. I am so blessed and thankful for my family, my life, and my business. Only speak blessings over your life and your business.

Affirmations

- I am worthy of great success.
- I can see myself winning day in and day out.
- I will use my words wisely to reach my goals.
- I will hold myself accountable for the decisions that I make in my business the good ones and the bad ones.
- I will only speak blessings out of my mouth every day.

God, I know my tongue often gets ahead of my mind and my heart. Sometimes I may be too quick to speak, but Lord Jesus help me to be quick to repent for the many thoughtless things that I have spoken. I am sorry if my words have caused me to fall short of your glory. Please help me to see when I am about to speak without thinking and to check my heart. Help me to be slow to speak. Help me Lord, to be a person full of loving words, full of the spirit, and overwhelmed with joy, love peace kindness and patience. Help me to have self-control over my tongue and to only speak positivity with my mouth over my life and my business in Jesus' name. Amen.

Reflections, Inspirations, & Strategies

_____

_____

_____

_____

_____

26

A KINGDOM BUSINESS

A kingdom business is a way of doing business that represents excellence and purpose. It is a business in which the nature and the characteristics are infused with the structure that God has for his kingdom. The fact that you run a profit-making business does not mean that it cannot be a ministry which impacts and transforms both saved and unsaved lives. Every believer should take every opportunity to witness to the lost and the broken. This is our mandate from God.

In Matthew 6:33 it says, "Seek ye first His kingdom and His righteousness and all these things shall be added unto you." If you plan to have a successful business, the very first thing that you should do is seek the kingdom of God. Seeking God on every decision that you make will save you a lot of bumps and bruises along the way.

Here are a few principles that I give my students on operating your business with kingdom principles:

1. Wait on God. This can be easier said than done. Allow yourself to be an open and willing vessel for God in your waiting. Try not to rush or make things fit that are not aligned with your purpose and your business. Be assured that even in the wait God is with you and it is all in his plans for you.

2. Choose Partners Wisely. Allow God to choose your life and your business partners who identify with your vision and who can carry your vision.

3. Honor God with your profits. Sowing and reaping are one of the main foundational

principles in the kingdom of God. Whatever you sow, that you shall also reap.

4. Focus on the development of people. Be committed to the development of your employees, your partners, your suppliers, and all of God's children. Not being consumed with greed and selfishness is key to getting what God has for you in your business. Give and it shall be given unto you, pressed down, shaken together, and running over. Give back and focus on the development of others.

5. Choose kingdom values. Operating your business under kingdom principles will carry you a long way. If you ever have a conflict between your business and business partners, operating in kingdom principles can be a great advantage to resolve problems.

Affirmations

- I put my faith and trust into God's hands.
- The word of God is with me each day.
- God's kingdom resides in my soul.
- My faith in God is growing with every breath I take.
- There is nothing that God and I cannot handle together.
- The Holy Spirit flows through me and my business is well.
- My business is doing exactly what it is supposed to do in this season as I operate in kingdom principles.

Lord Jesus, continued to lead and guide me as I operate the business that you have blessed me with. I know that as I walk with you and follow your lead, there is nothing that I cannot accomplish. Lord help me to continue to build my business on kingdom principles and a strong firm foundation through the word of God. Allow the Holy Spirit to lead and guide me every day as I put others before my own needs, God, because I know that you will meet every one of my needs. I believe in and trust you and I thank you for entrusting this business to me. In Jesus' name. Amen.

Reflections, Inspirations, & Strategies

_____
_____
_____
_____
_____
_____
_____
_____
_____
_____
_____
_____
_____
_____

27
BIBLICAL WEALTH AND PROSPERITY

Proverbs 10:22 says the blessings of the Lord bring wealth and He adds no trouble. Wealth is a gift from God and should only be viewed as that. Those of us who will be able to experience true biblical wealth understand this principle very well. When God blesses you, He blesses you to be a blessing to others and to carry out His work in the kingdom of God. Nothing more. Nothing less. Your wealth should never be used as a weapon or bragging, or to boast, or to bring others down and make them feel bad about the place that they are in God. God wants you to prosper. He will make you prosperous if you are willing to give up trying to achieve wealth your way. It isn't something that you can do alone. Biblical prosperity comes by following Luke 6:38 Give, and you will receive. Your gift will return to you in full pressed down, shaken together to make room for more, running over, and poured into your lap. The amount you give will determine the amount you get back. It's the easiest principal you can follow as an entrepreneur I challenge you on today to become a giver try God at his word and watch how the blessings begin to rain down on you. Repeat this I am a serial giver and what I make happen for others God will make happen for me. You are the favor that someone has been praying for so exercise your right to bless others and give cheerfully.

Affirmations

- Every day, my income is growing.
- My life is flowing with wealth and abundance.
- I am ready to receive wealth into my life.
- Money comes to me from all areas.
- I will experience great biblical wealth in my business in Jesus' name.

*L*ord Jesus help me to always recognize and understand that every blessing for my business and my life will consistently and always come from you. Help me to always be thankful for the small things and the small victories that we will win together. I give you all the praise for allowing me to be a vessel to build biblical wealth for myself and my family I will always be careful to give you the praise and to give what is due unto you in Jesus' name. Amen.

Reflections, Inspirations, & Strategies

_____

_____

_____

_____

_____

_____

_____

_____

_____

28

SUBMIT YOUR WORK UNTO THE LORD

When we respond to God in total surrender, it calls for humility and obedience. Submitting is saying, here I am Lord. Use me as you will. Submitting your life and your business unto the Lord will be the greatest thing that you could ever do. What that means is you are giving God total control over your life and your business. What better conductor can you ever have than the King of kings and the Lord of lords. When you submit, you will embrace the spirit of the humble dove and that gives you and the Lord a workable relationship.

When we submit to God, we allow God to transform our hearts and renew our minds, so that we can take on the character of God. One of the greatest spiritual truths in submission is it gives us unlimited access to the throne of God. It allows us to come to the Father and ask what we may. When you are an entrepreneur, you will have to ask the Lord for quite a few things, so having a workable and close relationship with God is imperative for your success. Submit your life and your business unto the Lord, so you can be blessed with exceeding blessings.

Affirmations

- Everything I do becomes a great success.
- I am accomplishing great things.
- Nothing will stop me from creating success.
- I am grateful for the great success in my life.
- Jesus loves me and his love lives in me.
- God is with me every day.
- I will yield all of my decisions for my business to God through prayer. He always works them out for me

Jesus, I accept your will, not my will, for my life and in my business. Teach and show me your ways and continue to lead and guide me when I am weary. I know that I can lean and depend on you. I submit my business and my life unto you. I ask that you continue to enlarge my territory and give me sound wisdom to operate. In Jesus' name. Amen.

Reflections, Inspirations, & Strategies

_____
_____
_____
_____
_____
_____
_____
_____
_____
_____
_____
_____
_____
_____
_____

29
YOU HAVE TO SOW IN ORDER TO GROW

Whatever you sow you will reap. Are you sowing seeds of negative thinking, lack of discipline, productiveness, greed, and dishonesty? If so, then that is exactly what you will get. If you sow seeds of money, generosity, discipline, thoughtfulness, affirming thoughts, and the Word of God, you will receive the same exact thing. Sowing and reaping are more than just monetary. It is in everything you do, say, and think.

Remember, it is not the size of the seed that makes it significant, but it is if what you are sowing is coming from your heart. When you have your greatest needs, that is when you should sow your greatest seeds. It's as simple as that.

Sometimes the return is quick, but other times it may take time. You must keep planting seeds daily, having full confidence that you will see a return in time. God's word never returns empty-handed and will accomplish exactly what it said it would do.

My prayer has always been Lord, make me the favor. That just means that I want to be in a place in my life where I can help as many people as possible and because of that, God has tremendously blessed me. My prayer for you is that God makes *you* the favor, that God opens up doors for you to be able to sow seed into those that need it so that you can continue to reap a harvest.

Affirmations

- Every seed that I have sown will return a hundredfold.
- I am a cheerful giver. Therefore, great wealth will come to me easily and effortlessly.
- God is opening the windows of heaven and pouring me out of blessing that I will not have room to receive.
- Every seed that I have sown will reap a harvest of exceeding blessings.

- I reap what I sow, and I sow joy peace and happiness to others.

I decree and declare that this day forward I will sow seeds that will add to my life. I will only engage in thoughts or deeds that will bring me and others abundance. I will sow cheerfully and willingly in the name of Jesus. I will keep a spirit of expectation knowing that God is not a man that he shall lie, and he will perform everything that he has promised me in Jesus' name. Amen.

Reflections, Inspirations, & Strategies

_____
_____
_____
_____
_____
_____

30

YOU WILL LOSE YOUR OIL AROUND THE FOOLISH

You are only effective when God is directing you, not when you are operating outside of godly wisdom. It is important that in business you keep yourself in the hedge of protection regarding your business and your life. Making hasty moves or foolish moves can not only destroy your business but destroy everything you have worked for in your life.

Seeking godly wisdom and godly counsel is always imperative when making big business decisions. God has a way of always releasing wisdom and instructions through many different avenues. You must listen to the still, small voice of the Holy Spirit for direction in your business. Having the oil of the Lord on your life and your business will not only propel you to be successful, but it will keep you protected. The oil of the Lord is the protection, guidance, and wisdom of the Holy Spirit. You are anointed to do just what God has called you to do it do not waste your oil on the foolish. Here are things to avoid at all cost.

1. Operating in greed looking for ways to make more money when you have not perfected avenues you already have going.
2. Making bad personal decisions. Your personal life will affect your business seek Godly trusted wisdom in all major decisions.
3. Never take on more clients than you can effectively manage. It's not quantity but quality.

Affirmations

- I will trust in the Lord with all my heart and not lean into my own understanding.
- I want to reach my God designed destiny.
- God blesses me every day with peace and always gives me strength.

- I will no longer cast my pearls to the swine but wait on God for divine direction.
- I will make wise decisions regarding who I allow in my life.

*J*esus, I thank you that you have all authority over everything in my life Lord. I thank you that just as the oil flowed from Aaron's beard, it will flow over my life and my business in the name of Jesus. Lord, continue to give me wisdom and power and allow me to heed to the voice of the Holy Spirit in the name of Jesus. Remove the scales from my eyes and my ears so that I see the plan that you have for my life in Jesus' name. Amen.

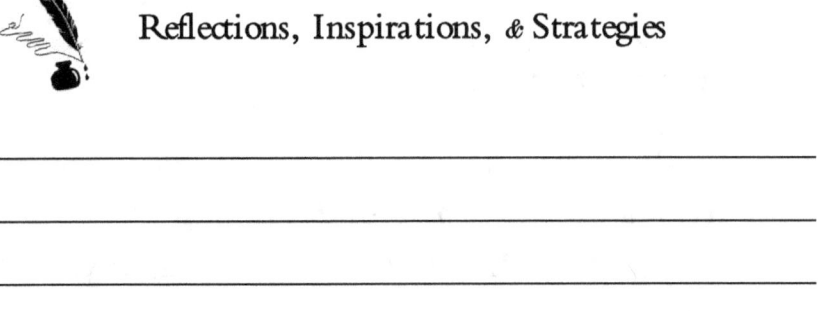

Reflections, Inspirations, & Strategies

_____
_____
_____
_____

Bea Great!

"Never underestimate the power of dreams and the influence of the human spirit. We are all the same in this notion: The potential for greatness lives within each of us." — *Wilma Rudolph*

DAILY AFFIRMATIONS

CONFIDENCE AFFIRMATIONS

- I am happy.
- I am successful.
- I am healthy.
- I attract abundance.
- I have a great body.
- I deserve good things.
- Life is beautiful.
- I am confident.
- I am courageous.
- I am financially abundant.

POSITIVE AFFIRMATIONS

- I can do anything I want.
- I believe in myself.
- I can overcome anything I put my mind to.
- I am bold and courageous.
- I am good at anything I put my mind to.
- I can overcome any obstacle.

- People are attracted to my self-confidence.
- I embrace challenges as opportunities.
- I can take on any challenge.
- I am ready to take on the world.
- Every day I take action and move forward in my life.
- Nothing will stop me from succeeding.

Be encouraged throughout your day. Know that God is with you and he will never leave you. Decree and declare that all things are working together for your good. Continue to press your way and God will continue to make a way for you. You have everything you need in you to be a great success.

Repeat this: My business is renewed daily, and no weapon formed against it shall prosper. I am walking in prosperity and everything I touch is drenched in the oil of the Lord. All I do is win! Favor and blessings stalk me and the overflow reigns in my life. Greatness is my daily portion and nothing will stop me from accomplishing my dreams. I am called to BEA GREAT!

~BIBLE PROMISES~

CONFIDENCE

Be my rock of refuge, to which I can always go; give the command to save me, for you are my rock and my fortress. Deliver me, my God, from the hand of the wicked, from the grasp of those who are evil and cruel. For you have been my hope, Sovereign Lord, my confidence since my youth. **Psalm 71:3-5 NIV**

GUIDANCE

The Lord directs the steps of the godly. He delights in every detail of their lives. Though they stumble, they will never fall, for the Lord holds them by the hand. **Psalm 37:23-24 NLT**

PROVISION

And God is able to bless you abundantly, so that in all things at all times, having all that you need, you will abound in every good work. **2 Corinthians 9:8 NIV**

WISDOM

If any of you lacks wisdom, you should ask God, who gives generously to all without finding fault, and it will be given to you. **James 1:5 NIV**

THANKFULNESS

If any of you lacks wisdom, you should ask God, who gives generously to all without finding fault, and it will be given to you. **2 CORINTHIANS 9:15 NIV**

PERSEVERANCE

Consider it pure joy, my brothers and sisters, [a] whenever you face trials of many kinds, because you know that the testing of your faith produces perseverance. Let perseverance finish its work so that you may be mature and complete, not lacking anything. **James 1:2-4 ESV**

For Booking and speaking engagements email Kingdomstreetzconsulting@gmail.com or call (318)-600-5997

www.ingramcontent.com/pod-product-compliance
Lightning Source LLC
Chambersburg PA
CBHW071412210526
45465CB00001B/349